I0821391

# START HERE. START NOW...

START ANYWHERE!

# START HERE. START NOW...

## START ANYWHERE!

A JOURNAL TO DISCOVER YOUR BEST YEAR YET

RONNIE WALTER

CORAL GABLES

Published by Mango Publishing Group, a division of Mango Media Inc.

Cover, Layout & Design: © Ronnie Walter



For permission requests, please contact the publisher at:
Mango Publishing Group
2850 S Douglas Road, 2nd Floor
Coral Gables, FL 33134 USA
info@mango.bz

For special orders, quantity sales, course adoptions and corporate sales, please email the publisher at sales@mango.bz. For trade and wholesale sales, please contact Ingram Publisher Services at customer.service@ingramcontent.com or +1.800.509.4887.

Start Here, Start Now...Start Anywhere!: A Fill-In Journal to Discover Your Best Year Yet

Library of Congress Cataloging-in-Publication number: 2019954684
ISBN: (print) 978-1-64250-261-9, (ebook) 978-1-64250-262-6
BISAC category code SEL009000SELF-HELP / Creativity

Printed in the United States of America

# INTRODUCTION

People say that 80 per cent of success is just showing up and well, I have found that to be true! Getting started and staying focused on the true meaning of what you want to accomplish is half the battle, right? It's why those perky guests on the morning programs tell us to "keep our running shoes next to the bed" so we can jump-start our mornings without thinking about it.

Or if you're like me, you can use those shoes to sprint out to the coffee machine!

No matter what you want to do—develop a new habit or start a creative practice, a business, even a new health regime—finding confidence and sustaining enthusiasm can be tough. It's been proven, however, that putting thoughts down on paper has huge benefits for both your attitude and your behavior.

How cool is that? By simply taking the time to write down things, such as the day's experiences, favorite memories, personal reflections, or whatever you want to write, we can change the way we live our lives.

So why doesn't everybody do it? Well, there's that getting started thing. But don't worry, you have help! I've designed this journal with exactly that process in mind. It's a guide to writing down how you are feeling in this adventure called life, and that can keep you moving in the direction you want to go.

Some of the pages are dcsigned to help you see what you bring to the table, like your strengths and things that put a spring in your step (which of course you want more of). Others may be about obstacles, likes and dislikes, or goals and lists of steps you can take to accomplish those goals.

And here's the good part: you can fill in any of the pages any time you want, depending on how you feel and what you need. Plus there is ample space for "free-writing" or recording your thoughts of the day.

And there's no pressure because it's ALL good; journal writing benefits us in so many ways including stress reduction, increased mindfulness, recognition of patterns and ideas, and more. I can assure you it works. Keeping a journal regularly has helped my own busy "monkey mind" become calmer and more relaxed while I work toward my goals. And many a new idea has sprouted while writing out words on a blank piece of paper.

My wish is that *Start Here, Start Now…Start Anywhere* brings you an increased sense of your gifts, your talents, and some clarity around your goals. And if you don't have a clear picture of what that goal is right now (or like me, you have lots of them), regularly filling out this journal will help you discover where your heart lives—and that is when the magic happens!

***-Ronnie***

P.S. This book can also be colored in! If you choose to color your pages, keep in mind that some markers can bleed through to the next page so I would suggest using colored pencils for your best result.

This book belongs to:

________________________________________

GOALS
IDEAS
Dreams
PASSION
Inspiration
GROWTH
Curiosity
The
JOURNEY
is the
REWARD

## Write down 5 things that are awesome about you!

1 ........................................................................

........................................................................

2 ........................................................................

........................................................................

3 ........................................................................

........................................................................

4 ........................................................................

........................................................................

5 ........................................................................

........................................................................

# People tell me I'm...

ANYTHING
IS
POSSIBLE

What are some of the dreams you've had in the past (even when you were very young)?

What are some things that scare you? Why?

1. ..................................................

..................................................

..................................................

..................................................

..................................................

2. ..................................................

..................................................

..................................................

..................................................

..................................................

3. ..................................................

..................................................

..................................................

..................................................

..................................................

Balance
takes
PRACTICE

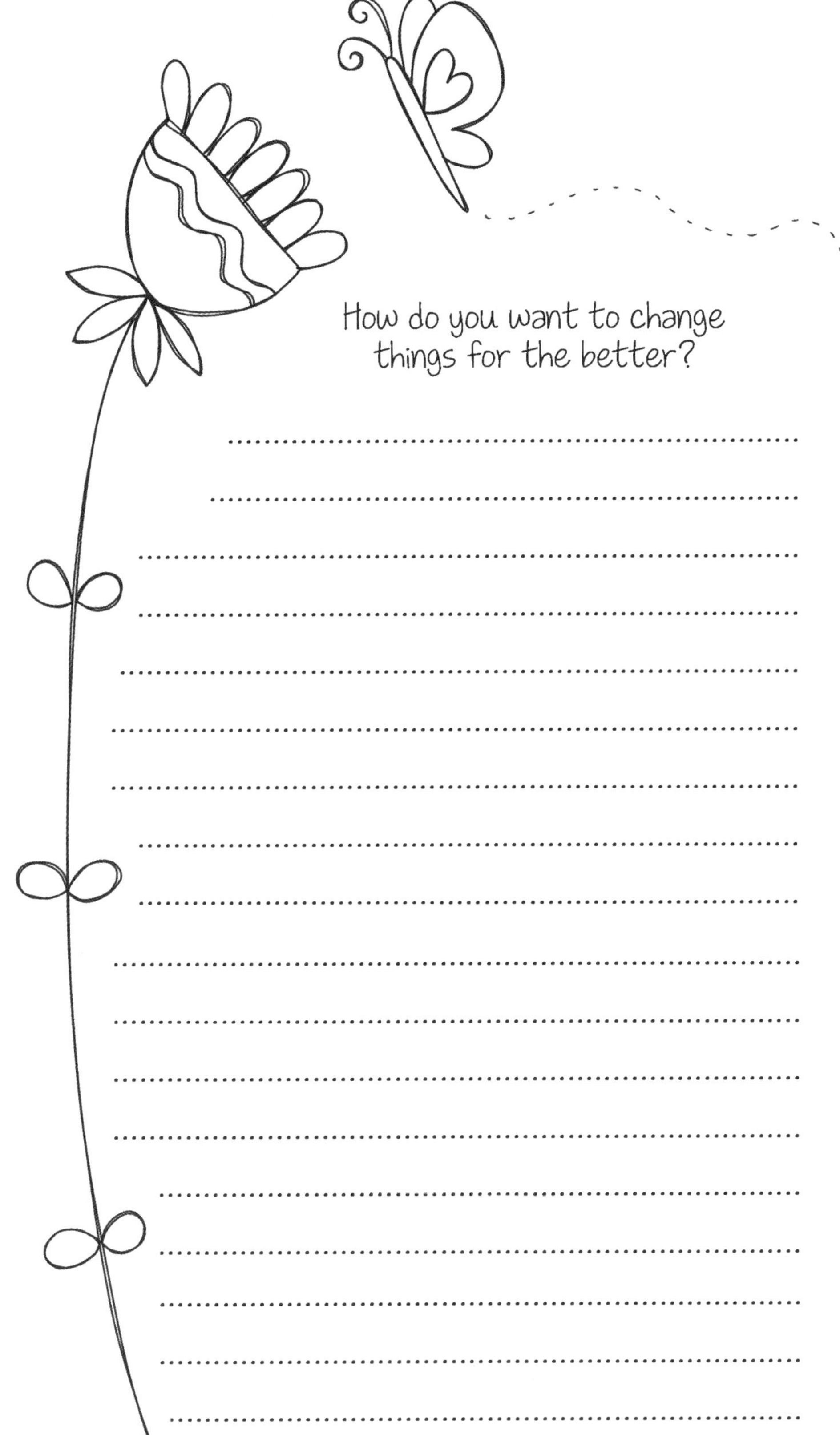

How do you want to change things for the better?

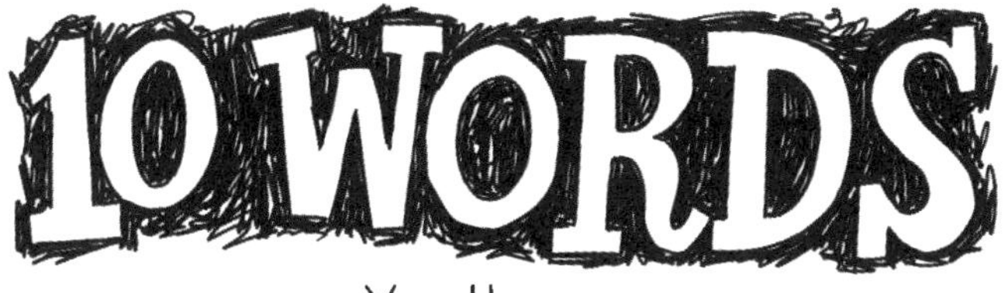


You like:

1. ..............................................................................................

2. ..............................................................................................

3. ..............................................................................................

4. ..............................................................................................

5. ..............................................................................................

6. ..............................................................................................

7. ..............................................................................................

8. ..............................................................................................

9. ..............................................................................................

10. ..............................................................................................

Your future self has written you a letter one year from now! Read about all the wonderful things you've accomplished in the next 365 days!

JUST BE YOUR
BEAUTIFUL
Self

How are you feeling right now?

## WRITE IT OUT!

Doesn't that feel better?
BETTER?

# I BELIEVE...

You are
UNIQUE
because...

Note to self:
It's not SELFISH
to be STRONG!

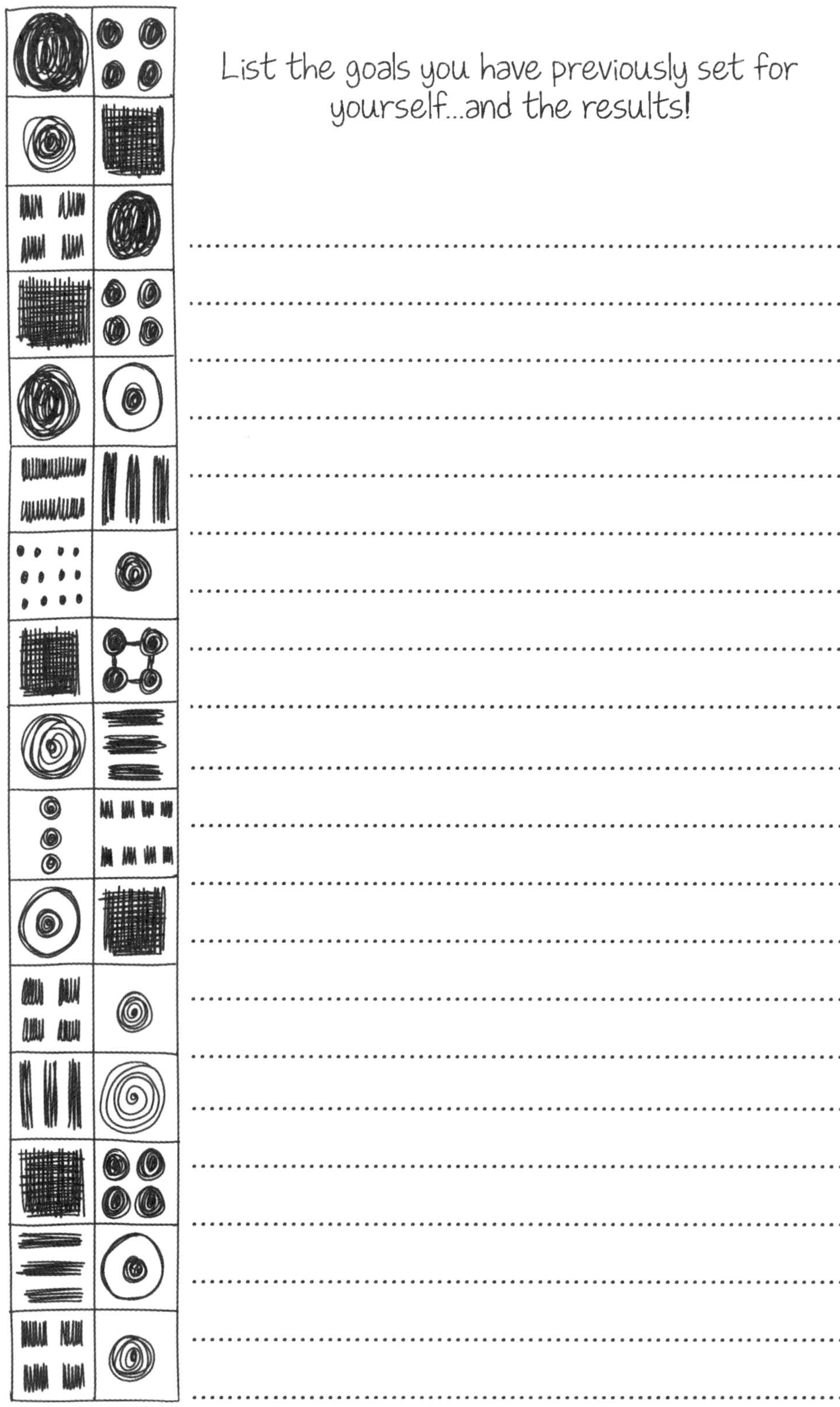

List the goals you have previously set for yourself...and the results!

See what you can do? What were the qualities that helped you succeed?

TRUST
YOUR
CRAZY
DREAMS

# What Keeps You Up At Night?

I want a whole lot more of this...

...and a whole lot less of this!

## People come to you to help them...

Write a letter to your present self from yourself ten years from now. Look at all the exciting things ahead just waiting for you!

Start
WHERE
YOU ARE

What are three skills you perform that you don't even think about?
1
2
3

IMAGINE

## What could you talk about for hours?

Thoughts, feelings, rants, and opinions!

You've Got This!

I am so grateful for these gifts in my life!

Be True
Be You

# JUST *for* TODAY…

I WILL

These are things that inspire me:

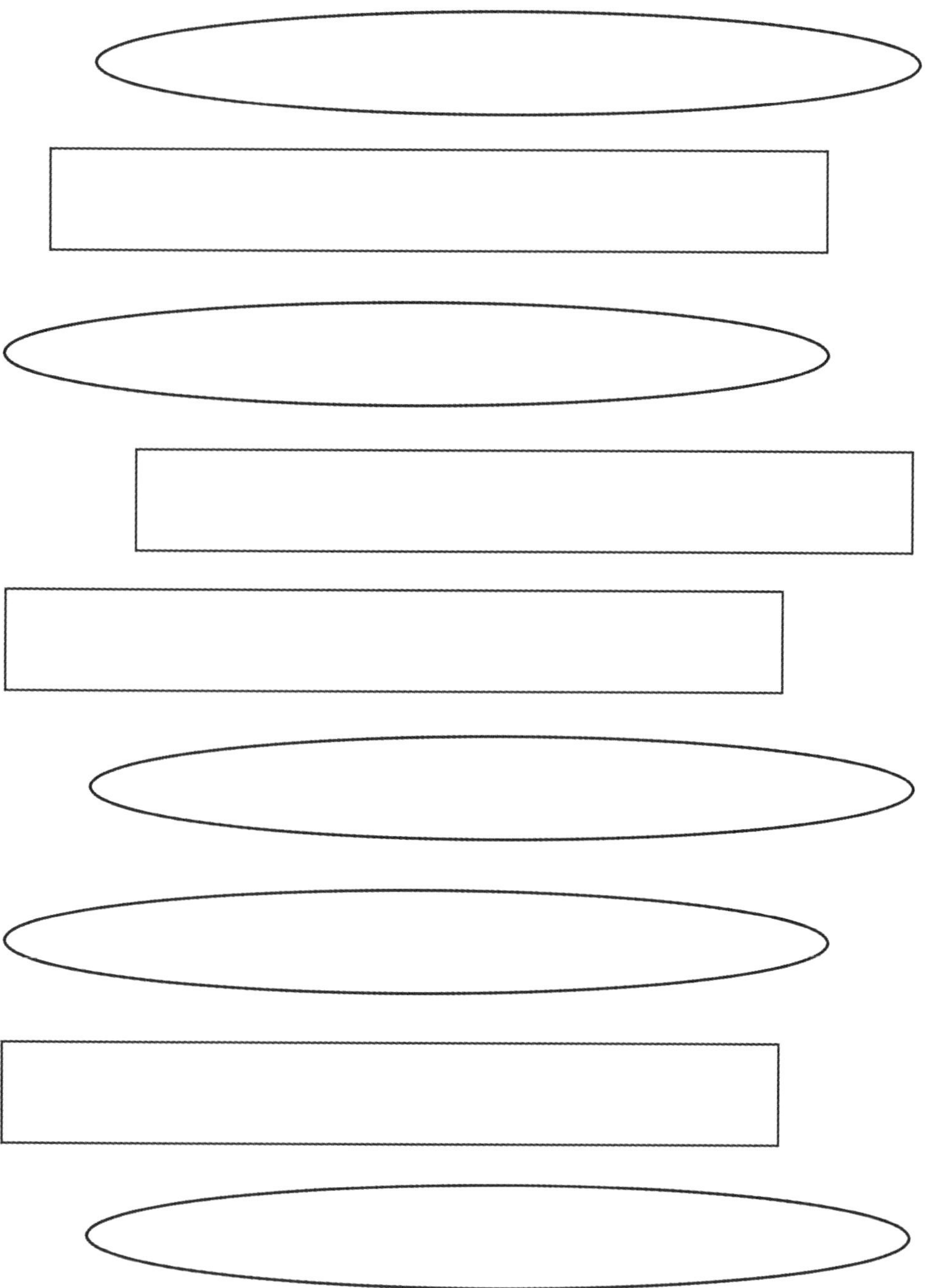

What makes you different makes you beautiful

When I need help or support, I can reach out to these amazing people in my life.

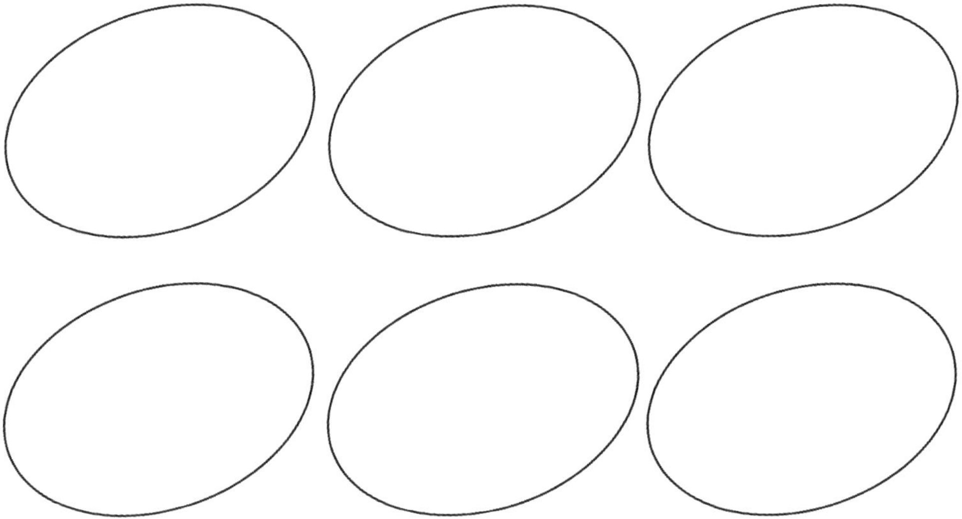

If I had all the money I ever needed, these are things I would do each day:

1 ..............................................................
..............................................................

2 ..............................................................
..............................................................

3 ..............................................................
..............................................................

4 ..............................................................
..............................................................

5 ..............................................................
..............................................................

* Can I do any of these things today?

Just
Breathe

I AM SO...

# What's Your SECRET Wish*?

*or that idea you just can't get out of your head!

Simply Begin Again
12
11
1
10
2
9
3
8
4
7
5
6
There's Still Time

# WHAT IS GOING WELL RIGHT NOW?

What are three things you could stop doing (immediately if you can) to make room for the things you really want?

These are the things that other people tell me I'm good at... the kinds of things that if someone compliments me on it, I respond with a shrug and a "no biggie"!

Hint: These things often turn out to be the "biggies"!

Follow YOUR BLISS

Things that make me happy

What are 3 Things You can't live without?

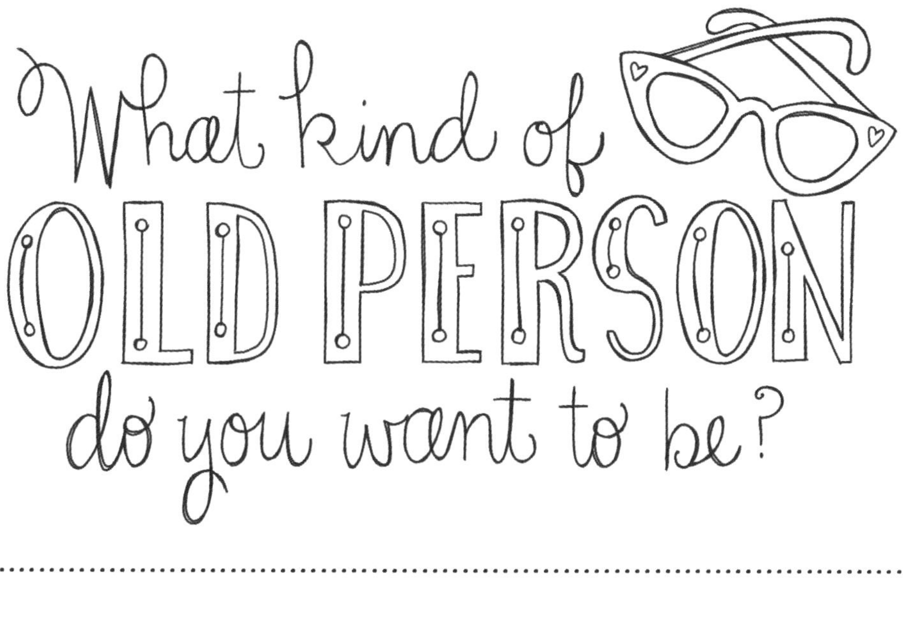


ECCENTRIC? OPINIONATED? WACKY?

WISE? CRANKY? WARM & FUZZY?

LIVE
YOUR
STORY.

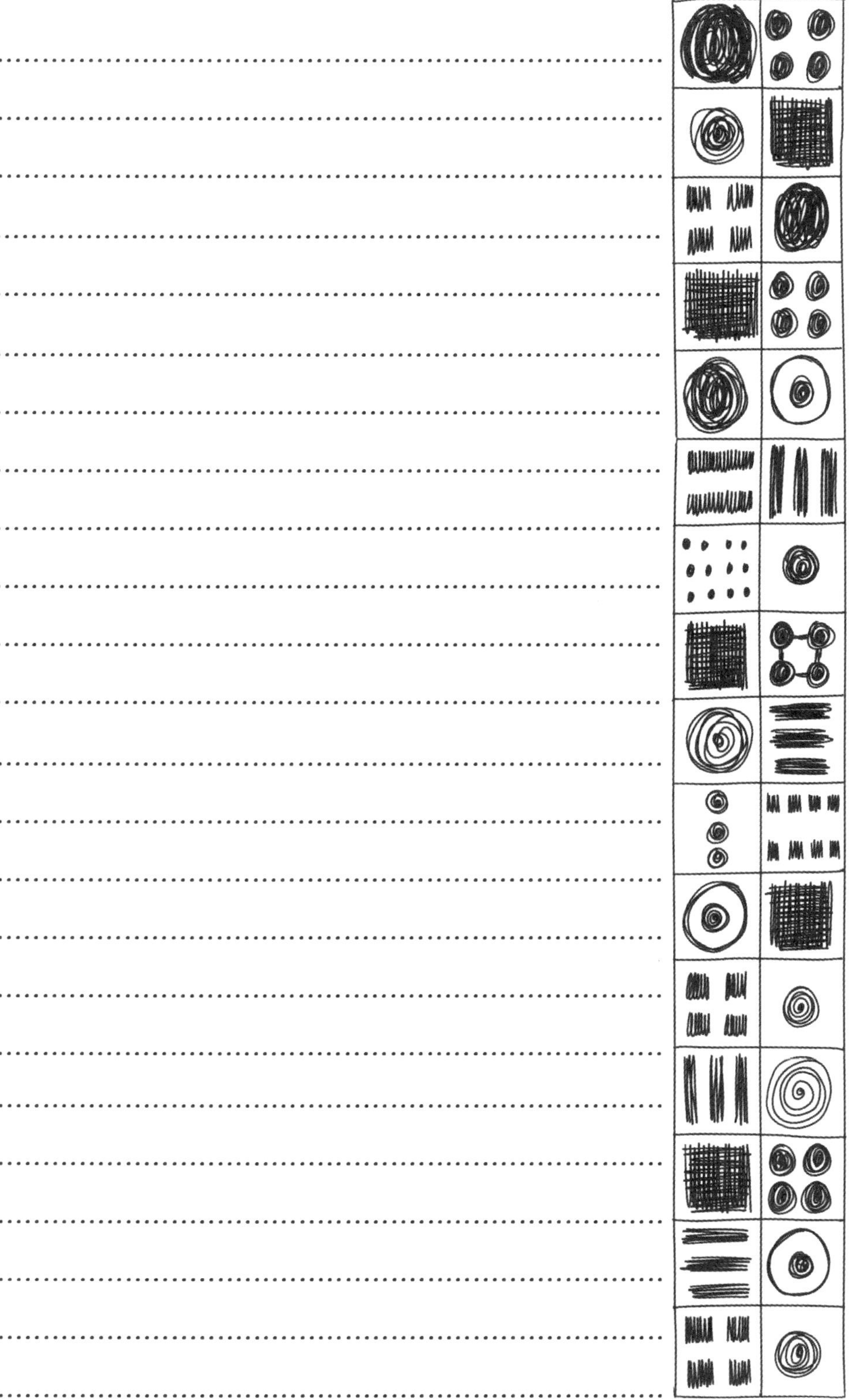

Things that I love...

# DESCRIBE YOUR IDEA OF SUCCESS

I wish I were better at...

You just won an Award!
WHAT IS IT FOR?
1st

# THIS IS NOT A TO-DO LIST...
# IT'S A Ta-Daaa! LIST*

..........................................................................................

..........................................................................................

..........................................................................................

..........................................................................................

..........................................................................................

..........................................................................................

..........................................................................................

..........................................................................................

..........................................................................................

..........................................................................................

..........................................................................................

..........................................................................................

..........................................................................................

..........................................................................................

*BIG & SMALL MOMENTS TO CELEBRATE

What makes you feel valued?
How could you feel that way more often?

Take Time To
Celebrate
Every small
step toward
your goal
is worth
celebrating!

To me...
HAPPINESS
looks like...

YES
and
YES

Chill out
Reflect
UNWIND
relax

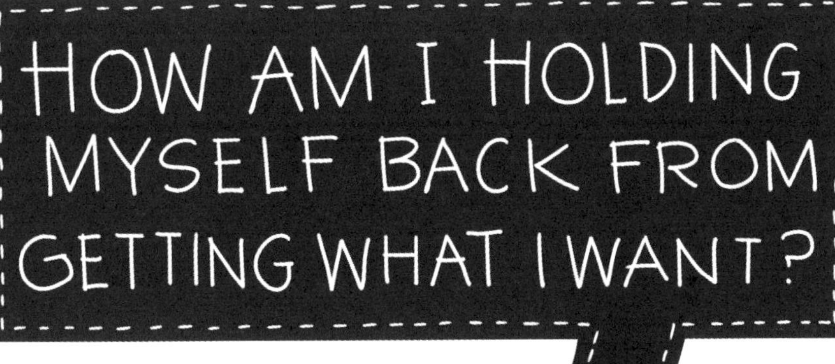
HOW AM I HOLDING MYSELF BACK FROM GETTING WHAT I WANT?

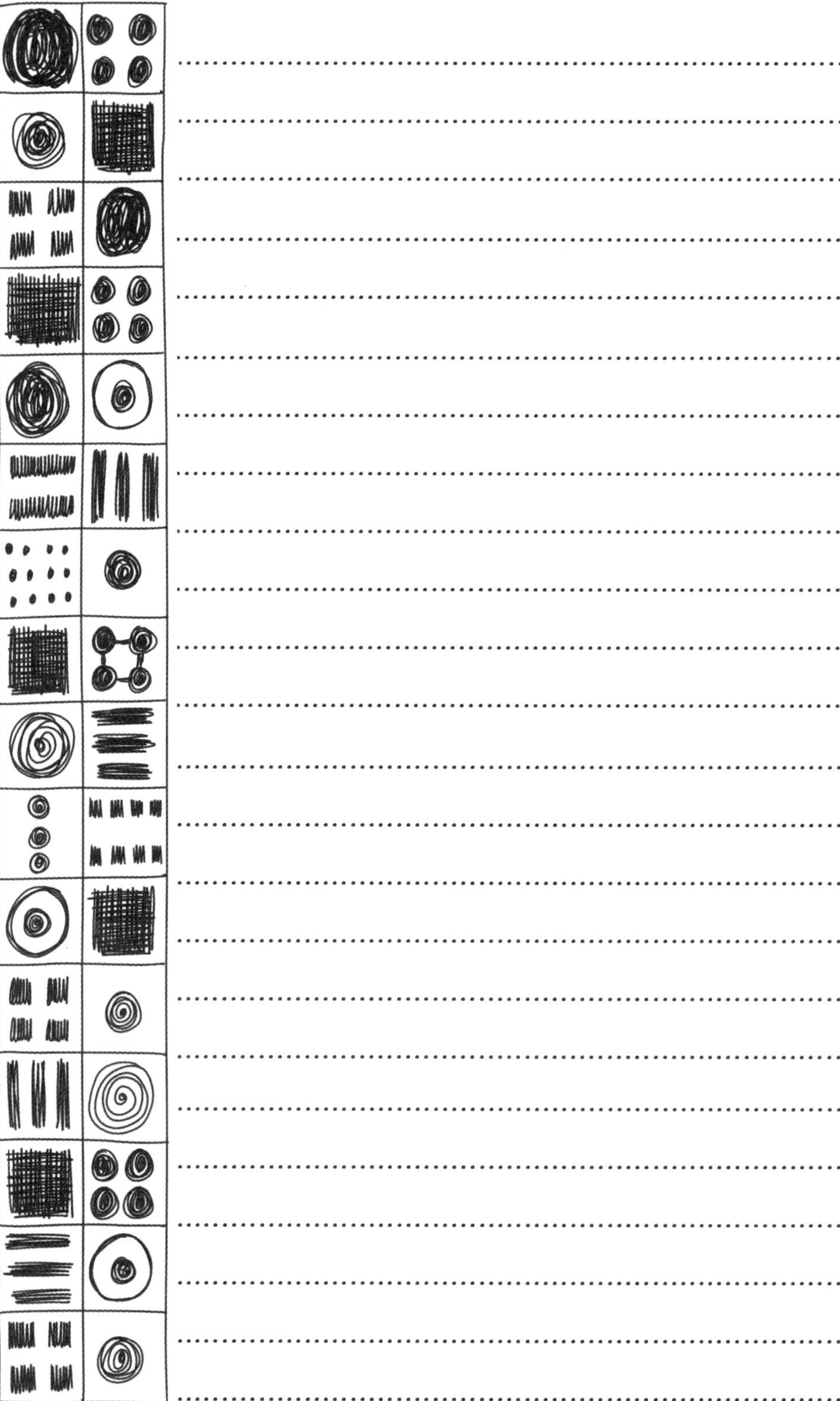

# Write a THANK YOU NOTE!

Dear Me,

To:

Love, me

Keep it

SIMPLE

BOOKS
I WANT TO READ

- [ ] ..............................
- [ ] ..............................
- [ ] ..............................
- [ ] ..............................
- [ ] ..............................
- [ ] ..............................
- [ ] ..............................
- [ ] ..............................
- [ ] ..............................
- [ ] ..............................
- [ ] ..............................
- [ ] ..............................

# MY IDEAL DAY LOOKS A LOT LIKE THIS!

morning

mid-day

afternoon

evening

night-time

Positive
Vibes
Only

Three goals I'd like to achieve in the next year:

One...

Two...

Three...

GOAL
GETTER

WHAT Lights ME UP?

GO
YOUR
own
WAY

Write a letter from your future 100-year-old self, letting the "present you" know what you experienced and accomplished. Did your 100-year-old self share any wisdom that you can apply to your life right now?

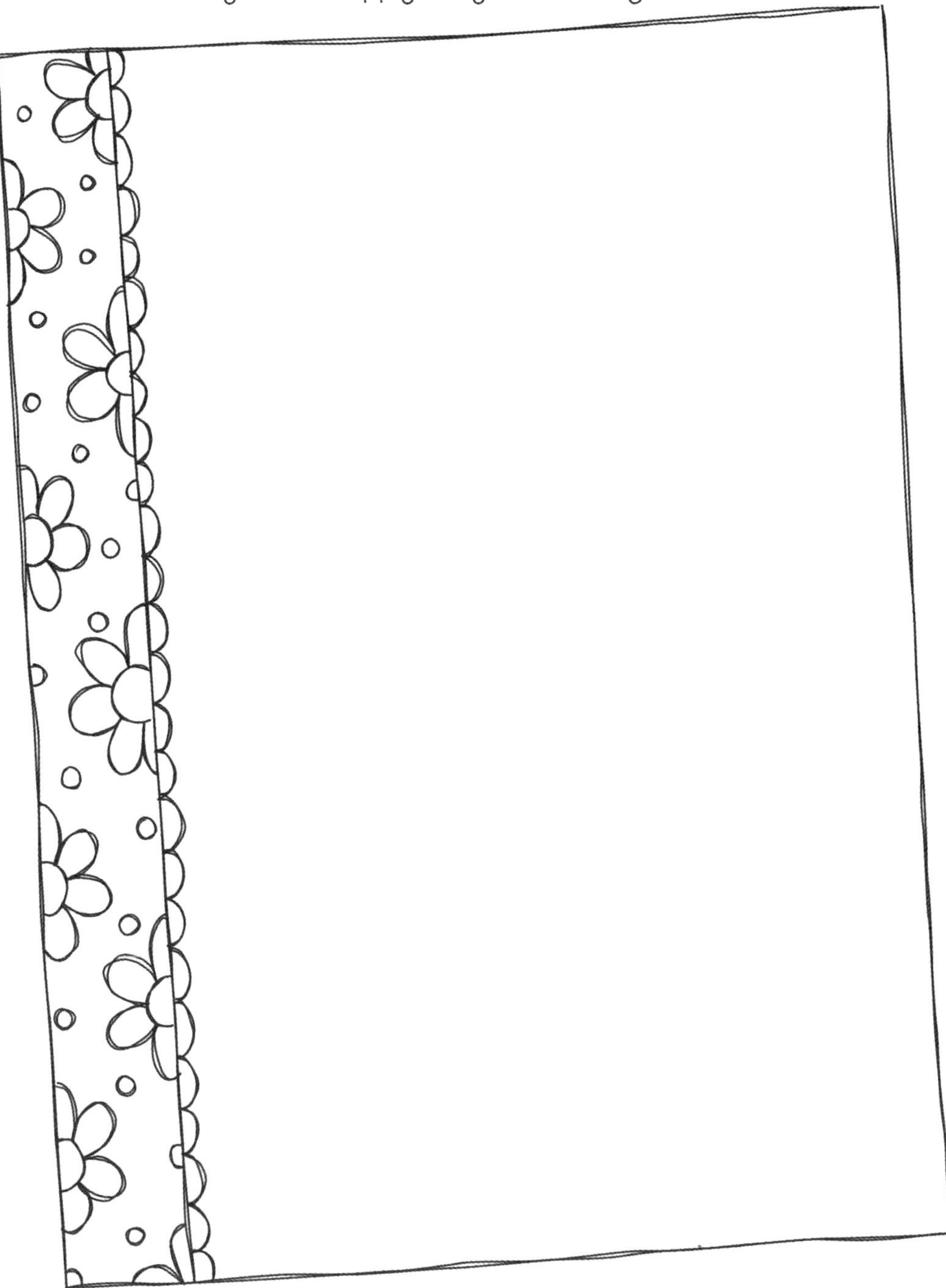

YOU ARE
STRONGER
THAN YOU THINK AND
MORE
POWERFUL
THAN YOU KNOW.

Where are you happiest?

You were born to
SHINE!

I, ____________________
(your name here)
AM
ENOUGH!

# ABOUT THE AUTHOR

Ronnie Walter is an artist and award-winning writer. As a professional illustrator she has licensed her designs onto hundreds of products including stickers, greeting cards, stationery, giftware, home goods, fabric, and more. She is the creative force behind the bestselling Coloring Café® series of adult coloring books, the author of *Gratitude with Attitude: How Journaling Thankfulness for 5 Minutes a Day Can Change Your Life* and has published both business and fiction books about the artist's life.

Ronnie is also a teacher and coach for artists and creatives, helping them to clarify their goals and move their creative dreams and businesses forward. She lives in a little house by the water with her husband Jim Marcotte and the best shelter dog ever, Larry.

Mango Publishing, established in 2014, publishes an eclectic list of books by diverse authors—both new and established voices—on topics ranging from business, personal growth, women's empowerment, LGBTQ studies, health, and spirituality to history, popular culture, time management, decluttering, lifestyle, mental wellness, aging, and sustainable living. We were recently named 2019's #1 fastest growing independent publisher by *Publishers Weekly*. Our success is driven by our main goal, which is to publish high quality books that will entertain readers as well as make a positive difference in their lives.

Our readers are our most important resource; we value your input, suggestions, and ideas. We'd love to hear from you—after all, we are publishing books for you!

Please stay in touch with us and follow us at:

Facebook: Mango Publishing
Twitter: @MangoPublishing
Instagram: @MangoPublishing
LinkedIn: Mango Publishing
Pinterest: Mango Publishing

Sign up for our newsletter at www.mango.bz and receive a free book!

Join us on Mango's journey to reinvent publishing, one book at a time.